European Colonies in the Americas

French Colonies in the Americas

Lewis K. Parker

French Colonies in the Americas
Copyright © 2002 by Rosen Book Works, Inc.

On Deck™ Reading Libraries
Published by Rigby
a division of Reed Elsevier Inc.
1000 Hart Road
Barrington, IL 60010-2627
www.rigby.com

Book Design: Erica Clendening
Text: Lewis K. Parker
Photo Credits: Cover, pp. 18–19 National Archives of Canada/
C-17875; C-77769; p. 4 Erica Clendening; pp. 5, 12, 13 © Hulton/
Archive/Getty Images; pp. 6–7 © Metropolitan Toronto Reference
Library/T31616; pp. 8, 11, 15, 18 (inset) © North Wind Picture Archives;
p. 9 © Index Stock; p. 9 (inset) © Corbis; p. 10 © Bettmann/Corbis;
pp. 16–17 © American Illustrators Gallery, NYC/www.amerillus.com/
Bridgeman Art Library; p. 20 © Wolfgang Kaehler/Corbis

On Deck™ is a trademark of Reed Elsevier Inc.

11 10 09 08
10 9 8 7 6 5 4 3

Printed in China

ISBN-10: 0-7578-2425-0
ISBN-13: 978-0-7578-2425-8

Contents

The First French Explorers

In 1524, King Francis I of France sent Giovanni da Verrazzano *(gee-oh-VAH-nee duh vehr-uh-ZA-noh)* to explore the east coast of North America.

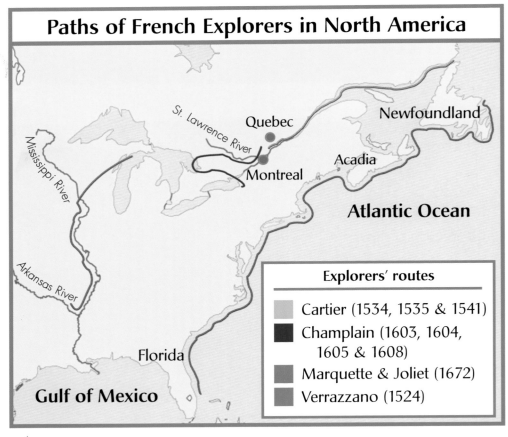

Paths of French Explorers in North America

St. Lawrence River

Quebec

Newfoundland

Mississippi River

Acadia

Montreal

Atlantic Ocean

Arkansas River

Florida

Gulf of Mexico

Explorers' routes

Cartier (1534, 1535 & 1541)
Champlain (1603, 1604, 1605 & 1608)
Marquette & Joliet (1672)
Verrazzano (1524)

Verrazzano explored the coast from Florida to Newfoundland, Canada. He claimed land that is now Canada for France.

A few years later, the king sent Jacques Cartier *(JHAHK kar-tee-AY)* to explore North America.

Cartier made three trips to North America between 1534 and 1541. He was the first European person to explore the Gulf of St. Lawrence.

Early Settlements

In 1604, France set up its first lasting colony in the Americas. The colony was called Acadia *(uh-KAY-dee-uh)*. It was in the eastern part of Canada. All of the French colonies in the Americas would come to be known as New France.

The French sent many people to explore Canada.

In 1608, Samuel de Champlain founded the settlement of Quebec (kwih-BEHK) on the St. Lawrence River. Champlain set up a trading post and built farms nearby. Champlain was friendly with some Native American tribes that lived near Quebec. He traded with them and hoped they would help him explore new land. A few years later, French fur traders set up more settlements along the St. Lawrence River.

Samuel de Champlain was nicknamed the "Father of New France" because he started French settlements in New France.

Champlain drew this map showing some of the places he visited in New France.

Champlain was one of the first Europeans to write about Niagara Falls.

By 1660, only a few thousand French settlers lived in all of New France. King Louis XIV of France sent thousands of new settlers to the colonies to help New France grow.

King Louis XIV gave land in New France to businesspeople and army officers who wanted to settle there.

Many French people went to Canada to get rich by trading furs. The furs were sent back to Europe where they were made into fur hats. This trapper is wearing a hat made from fur. Beaver hats were very popular in Europe.

In 1672, Louis Joliet *(LOO-ee jhawl-YAY)* and Jacques Marquette *(JHAHK mar-KEHT)* found the headwaters of the Mississippi River.

Joliet and Marquette explored the Mississippi River hoping to find a way to reach the Pacific Ocean and the Far East.

Then, other French explorers followed the river to the Gulf of Mexico and claimed the Mississippi River Valley for France.

Pierre Le Moyne

In 1699, Pierre Le Moyne (pea-AYR luh MWOIN) *set up the colony of Louisiana near the Gulf of Mexico. By 1731, there were about 8,000 people living in Louisiana. The French built many forts between Louisiana and the rest of New France.*

13

Living and Working in New France

Most of the early colonists in New France were men who were not married. They made their living by trading fur. After they got married, many became farmers. They raised livestock and grew wheat and oats. They also worked in the fishing and lumber businesses.

By the end of the 17th century, fur hats were no longer popular in Europe. Fewer furs were being sent to France from the French colonies in the Americas. Many fur traders in New France became farmers to earn money.

15

At War with England

As far back as the early 1600s, France and England fought over control of the land in New France. They also fought for control of the fur trade.

In 1754, a war began between France and England. The war started because the French had set up forts on land in the Ohio River Valley. The English colony of Virginia also claimed this land.

Fort Duquesne (doo-KAYN), built in 1754, was one of the forts the French built in the Ohio River Valley. The fort and the land around it later became the city of Pittsburgh.

After many years of fighting, the French lost the war in 1763. The English won the French lands in the Ohio River Valley and in Canada.

England sent many soldiers to fight the French settlers in the Ohio River Valley.

In 1759, the French and British fought a battle at Quebec. Four years later, the British won the war.

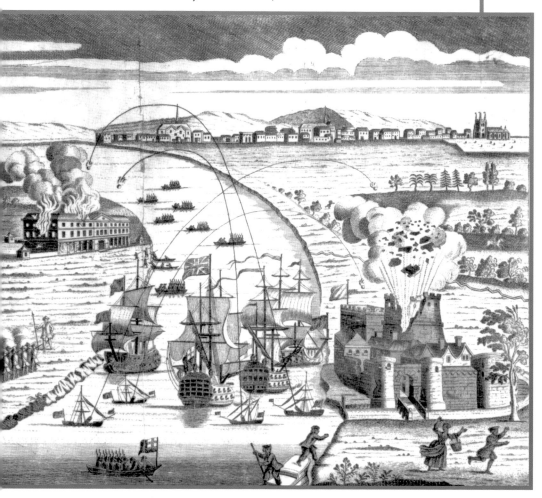

The End of New France

In 1803, France sold the rest of its land in New France to the United States. French colonies in the Americas only lasted about 150 years, but they changed the way the United States and Canada grew.

Canada has two official languages: French and English.

Montreal, Canada

TIME LINE

1524	Verrazzano explores North America for France.
1534–1541	Cartier makes three trips to North America.
1604	France sets up the colony of Acadia.
1608	Champlain starts the settlement of Quebec.
1665–1672	King Louis XIV sends thousands of people to New France to make the colonies bigger and better.
1672	Marquette and Joliet find the headwaters of the Mississippi River.
1699	Le Moyne sets up the colony of Louisiana.
1754	France and England go to war over New France.
1763	France loses the Ohio River Valley and Canada to England.
1803	France sells Louisiana to the United States.

The Fact Box

Today, about six million people in Canada speak French. In the United States, there is still a large group of French-speaking people in Louisiana.

Glossary

Americas (uh-**mehr**-uh-kuhz) the name used when speaking about North America, South America, and Central America

colonists (**kahl**-uh-nihsts) people who live in a colony

colony (**kahl**-uh-nee) a faraway land that belongs to or is under the control of a nation

Europe (**yur**-uhp) one of the seven continents on Earth, where England, France, and Spain are found

explore (ehk-**splor**) to search for new places

explorers (ehk-**splor**-uhrz) people who search for new places

forts (**forts**) strong buildings or places that can be guarded easily

gulf (**guhlf**) a part of an ocean or sea that spreads into land

headwaters (**hehd**-waw-tuhrz) the beginnings of bodies of water, such as rivers

livestock (**lyv**-stahk) animals, such as horses and cows, raised on a farm

popular (**pahp**-yuh-luhr) liked by most people

settlement (**seht**-l-muhnt) a place where people come to live

settlers (**seht**-luhrz) people who come to stay in a new country or place

tribes (**trybz**) groups of people who share the same language and practices

Resources

Books

New France
by Robert Livesey
Stoddart Kids (1990)

Samuel de Champlain
by Liz Sonneborn
Franklin Watts (2001)

Web Site

Virtual Museum of New France
http://www.civilization.ca/vmnf/vmnfe.asp

Index